United States Government Accountability Office

Report to the Chairman, Subcommittee on Oversight and Management Efficiency, Committee on Homeland Security, House of Representatives

October 2013

FEDERAL FACILITIES

I0455242

Selected Facilities' Emergency Plans Generally Reflect Federal Guidance

GAO-14-101

GAO Highlights

Highlights of GAO-14-101, a report to the Chairman, Subcommittee on Oversight and Management Efficiency, Committee on Homeland Security, House of Representatives

FEDERAL FACILITIES

Selected Facilities' Emergency Plans Generally Reflect Federal Guidance

Why GAO Did This Study

Recent emergencies, such as earthquakes in the nation's capital, have raised concerns about how prepared federal agencies are in the 9,600 facilities owned or leased by GSA and protected by the Department of Homeland Security's FPS to safely evacuate occupants in federal buildings. All federal agencies are required to prepare OEPs for their facilities, which describe actions agencies should take to plan for a safe evacuation during an emergency.

GAO was asked to provide information on how prepared GSA-owned and -leased facilities are to evacuate occupants during an emergency. This report describes (1) who is responsible for ensuring that federal facilities have OEPs in place and the extent to which selected facilities' OEPs reflect federal guidance, and (2) the evacuation challenges, if any, selected facilities experienced and what actions, if any, they reported taking to address these issues.

GAO reviewed federal regulations and guidance on OEPs, including documents from ISC, GSA, and FPS, which develop governmentwide physical security standards and policies, such as minimum elements for OEPs. GAO also reviewed OEPs and interviewed facility officials at 20 GSA-owned and -leased facilities, selected based on geographic dispersion, recent evacuations, and facility security level. While not generalizable to all GSA-owned and -leased facilities the results provided perspectives of varying facilities.

DHS written and technical comments were incorporated, as appropriate. GSA did not have any comments.

View GAO-14-101. For more information, contact Joseph Kirschbaum at (202) 512-9971 or kirschbaumj@gao.gov or Mark Goldstein at (202) 512-2834 or goldsteinm@gao.gov .

What GAO Found

Federal agencies occupying facilities owned or leased by the General Services Administration (GSA) are responsible for preparing and maintaining occupant emergency plans (OEP), with assistance or guidance from the Federal Protective Service (FPS) and others, and the majority of selected federal facilities' OEPs GAO reviewed reflect federal guidance. As required by federal regulations, all 20 selected facilities had OEPs and had designated officials, who are responsible for maintaining OEPs and initiating action according to the OEP in the event of an emergency, including the evacuation of facility occupants. Consistent with federal guidance, officials at 19 of the 20 selected facilities reported that they review and update OEPs at least annually, and officials at 1 facility said they were in the process of updating their OEP. When requested, FPS provides OEP guidance, such as templates to facility officials. Officials at 14 facilities reported using FPS guidance or feedback for their OEPs, officials at 1 facility reported not using FPS guidance, and officials at 5 facilities said they used their own agency's guidance. FPS also checks OEPs during periodic facility security assessments— conducted at least every 3 to 5 years— to assess overall facility risk. GSA officials said they have a role in coordinating directly with facilities to provide guidance and feedback on OEPs, and to help facility officials plan drills and exercises. To assist agency officials as they develop OEPs that best fit individual facilities and agency needs, the Interagency Security Committee (ISC), a Department of Homeland Security–chaired policy development organization, in April 2010 identified 10 minimum elements, such as exercises or evacuating occupants with special needs, that should be addressed in an OEP. Thirteen of the 20 selected facilities addressed all 10 minimum elements in OEPs or related documents. Seven facilities' OEPs did not address at least 1 of the 10 elements; however, lack of an element does not necessarily indicate potential vulnerabilities for that facility because the intent of the element may be addressed by other procedures or modified based on facility characteristics. For example, evacuation exercises were not included in OEPs for 2 facilities located in leased GSA space; however, officials said they participate in drills conducted by building management. The 20 selected facility OEPs were unique to each facility and how OEPs addressed particular elements.

Officials at 14 of 20 facilities identified evacuation challenges. The most frequently cited challenges included employee apathy toward participating in drills, accounting for employees, and keeping contact information updated. Officials at all but one facility, which was updating its OEP, reported various ways they addressed evacuation challenges, including using technology such as entry scan systems and radios to track and communicate with employees and making evacuation training more interesting to employees. Other incidents and emerging threats also prompted officials to change OEPs or evacuation training. For example, during the 2011 Washington, D.C., earthquake, officials at selected facilities in the D.C. area said that the lack of employee training on earthquake procedures may have exposed employees to potential hazards when they self-evacuated. Officials reported revising their OEPs to include procedures for earthquakes. Recent shootings also prompted facility officials to revise their OEPs and participate in FPS awareness training on active shooter incidents. Officials at 6 facilities did not report challenges.

_____ United States Government Accountability Office

Contents

Abbreviations

DHS	Department of Homeland Security
EEOC	U.S. Equal Employment Opportunity Commission
FPS	Federal Protective Service
FSL	facility security level
GSA	General Services Administration
ISC	Interagency Security Committee
MIST	Modified Infrastructure Survey Tool
OEP	occupant emergency plan
REXUS	Real Estate Across the United States

GAO U.S. GOVERNMENT ACCOUNTABILITY OFFICE

441 G St. N.W.
Washington, DC 20548

October 25, 2013

The Honorable Jeff Duncan
Chairman, Subcommittee on Oversight
  and Management Efficiency
Committee on Homeland Security
House of Representatives

Dear Mr. Chairman:

Recent natural disasters, such as earthquakes in the nation's capital, and fatal attacks, such as the shooting at the Long Beach, California, federal building in February 2012, have raised concerns about emergency preparedness in approximately 9,600 facilities owned or leased by the General Services Administration (GSA) and protected by the Department of Homeland Security's (DHS) Federal Protective Service (FPS).[1] All federal agencies are required to prepare occupant emergency plans (OEP) for their facilities, which describe the actions that officials should take to plan for safe evacuations during an emergency.[2] The Interagency Security Committee (ISC)—a DHS-chaired interagency organization that develops government-wide physical security standards and is responsible for enhancing the protection of federal facilities—as well as GSA and FPS provide guidance to officials in GSA-owned and -leased facilities to assist in developing OEPs. Given the importance of safely evacuating federal employees and visitors from federal facilities in an emergency, you asked us to provide information on how prepared federal facilities owned and leased by GSA are to evacuate occupants during an emergency. This report describes (1) who is responsible for ensuring that GSA-owned and -leased facilities have OEPs in place and the extent to which selected facilities' OEPs reflect federal guidance, and (2) the evacuation challenges, if any, that selected facilities experienced and what actions, if any, they reported taking to address these issues.

---

[1]The Washington, D.C., area experienced a magnitude 3.6 earthquake on July 16, 2010, and a magnitude 5.8 earthquake on August 23, 2011. On February 16, 2012, agents at the U.S. Immigration and Customs Enforcement office in Long Beach were involved in a workplace violence incident; one was wounded and one killed.

[2]See 41 C.F.R. §§ 102-74.230 to .260.

To describe who is responsible for ensuring that OEPs are in place, we reviewed federal laws, regulations, executive orders, and guidance related to the oversight of federal facilities, and guidance issued for agencies by ISC, GSA, and FPS.[3] We also reviewed our previous work on the roles of ISC, GSA, and FPS in protecting federal properties.[4] We interviewed relevant senior officials from those three agencies regarding their agencies' role in ensuring that federal facilities have OEPs in place.

To determine the extent to which selected facilities' OEPs reflected federal guidance, we conducted site visits at 20 GSA-owned and -leased facilities in Washington, D.C.; Los Angeles, California; and Kansas City, Missouri.[5] We selected a nonprobability sample of facilities based on factors such as geographical dispersion and reporting of an evacuation incident in 2011 or 2012, as well as to reflect a mix of GSA-owned and -leased properties and facility security levels (FSL).[6] Appendix I contains a table of the characteristics of our 20 selected facilities. For each facility, we obtained the facility OEP and compared it with the 10 minimum elements that should be in an OEP, such as the circumstances for activating the OEP, based on *ISC's Physical Security Criteria for Federal*

---

[3]Among others, guidance we reviewed included the following: ISC, *Physical Security Criteria for Federal Facilities: An Interagency Security Committee Standard,* (Washington, D.C.: April 12, 2010) and *Occupant Emergency Programs: An Interagency Security Committee Guide* (Washington, D.C.; March 2013); FPS, *Secure Facilities, Safe Occupants–Occupant Emergency Plans: Development, Implementation and Maintenance,* Updated May 2010, and related supplements; and GSA's Public Buildings Service, *Occupant Emergency Program Guide,* (Washington, D.C.: March 2002).

[4]GAO, *Federal Real Property Security: Interagency Security Committee Should Implement a Lessons-Learned Process,* GAO-12-901 (Washington, D.C.: Sept. 10, 2012); *Federal Protective Service: Actions Needed to Resolve Delays and Inadequate Oversight Issues with FPS's Risk Assessment and Management Program,* GAO-11-705R (Washington, D.C.: July15, 2011); and *Homeland Security: Greater Attention to Key Practices Would Improve the Federal Protective Service's Approach to Facility Protection,* GAO-10-142 (Washington, D.C.: Oct. 23, 2009).

[5]GSA reported having over 9,600 assets, or 11 percent of all federal assets, in September 2012, which includes office buildings, courthouses, warehouses, laboratories, parking lots, and other properties. We selected facilities from the almost 7, 900 GSA office buildings, of which 7,301 are office spaces that GSA leases. For the purposes of this report, we use the term "facilities" to describe the 20 GSA assets in our sample. We selected these three cities to reflect geographically-diverse areas and a range of concentrations of GSA facilities.

[6]FPS assigns an FSL of I to V to facilities it protects. A higher-numbered FSL facility would be considered a higher security risk than a lower-numbered FSL facility.

Facilities: An Interagency Security Committee Standard, April 12, 2010 (ISC 2010 standard).[7] We used the ISC 2010 standard's suggested elements because ISC's 2013 guidance was not finalized when we conducted our work or available when the plans we reviewed were developed. ISC officials said the elements identified in the ISC 2010 standard are incorporated in the 2013 ISC guidance. The elements in the 2010 ISC standard are general in nature, as the same element may be addressed in various ways based on agency preferences and differences in facility characteristics, and all of the elements are not always applicable to every facility (e.g., if the facility did not have a child care facility). Because of the general nature of the elements, we assessed whether an element was present in a facility's OEP, not how comprehensively or thoroughly it was addressed. At each of the 20 facilities, we interviewed GSA property managers and officials from agencies who occupy the facility. In instances where a particular element was not identified in an OEP, we discussed with officials how that element related to the characteristics of the facility. While the findings from our 20 case studies are not generalizable to all GSA-owned and -leased facilities, they provide specific examples of how selected facilities have addressed emergency plan requirements and provide insights from a range of federal facilities.

To describe evacuation challenges and actions taken to address them, we interviewed officials with OEP responsibilities at the 20 selected facilities. We relied on officials' statements regarding what was considered a challenge and how such issues were resolved. Where available, we reviewed after-action reports documenting facility evacuation experiences. We discussed evacuation experiences and challenges with ISC, FPS, and GSA officials in Washington, D.C., and with FPS officials who are located in the three site visit areas. Our findings regarding what issues presented challenges and how such challenges could be resolved cannot be generalized to all GSA-owned and -leased facilities; however, they provided specific examples of issues

---

[7]ISC, *Physical Security Criteria for Federal Facilities: An Interagency Security Committee Standard.* While federal facility officials are required to follow the ISC Physical Security Criteria, the elements listed in the criteria are suggested because the language indicates that the elements "should be" included, recognizing that adjustments may be made as appropriate for the facility. ISC's 2013 Occupant Emergency Programs Guide expands on information that should be in an OEP.

encountered and how varying facilities addressed them. Further details of our scope and methodology are contained in appendix I.

We conducted this performance audit from August 2012 to October 2013 in accordance with generally accepted government auditing standards. Those standards require that we plan and perform the audit to obtain sufficient, appropriate evidence to provide a reasonable basis for our findings and conclusions based on our audit objectives. We believe that the evidence obtained provides a reasonable basis for our findings and conclusions based on our audit objectives.

Background

Federal agencies are required to have an occupant emergency program that establishes procedures for safeguarding lives and property during emergencies in their respective facilities.[8] According to ISC, an OEP is a critical component of an effective occupant emergency program. Further, these plans are intended to minimize the risk to personnel, property, and other assets within a facility by providing facility-specific response procedures for occupants to follow.

Several federal entities—ISC, GSA, and FPS—play a role in protection policy and programs for GSA-owned and -leased facilities.

ISC

Established by Executive Order 12977, ISC is an interagency organization chaired by DHS to enhance the quality and effectiveness of security in, and protection of, nonmilitary buildings occupied by federal employees for nonmilitary activities in the United States, among other things.[9] ISC includes members from 53 federal departments and agencies, including FPS and GSA. Under the executive order, ISC was directed to develop policies and standards that govern federal facilities' physical security efforts. As a part of its government-wide effort to develop physical security standards and improve the protection of federal facilities, it also provides guidance on OEPs. In its 2010 standard, ISC

---

[8]See 41 C.F.R. §§ 102-74.230 to .260.

[9]Exec. Order No. 12,977, 60 Fed. Reg. 54,411 (Oct. 19, 1995).

lists 10 elements that should be addressed at a minimum in an OEP, and states that the plan must be reviewed annually.[10]

GSA

As the federal government's landlord, GSA designs, builds, manages, and maintains federal facilities. Presidential Policy Directive 21 designates DHS and GSA as cosector-specific agencies for the government facilities sector, 1 of 16 critical infrastructure sectors.[11] In 2002, GSA issued its *Occupant Emergency Program Guide* to provide step-by-step instructions for agencies to use to meet federal regulatory requirements for OEPs.[12] GSA also served as chair and sponsor of ISC's working group that developed additional guidance for preparing OEPs.[13]

FPS

The Homeland Security Act of 2002 transferred FPS from GSA to the newly established DHS in March 2003, and required DHS to protect the buildings, grounds, and property that are under the control and custody of GSA and the persons on the property.[14] As part of an agreement between GSA and DHS, FPS provides law enforcement and related security services for GSA's approximately 9,600 facilities, which include—but are not limited to—responding to incidents and conducting facility security assessments.[15] Facility security assessments are conducted by FPS inspectors to help FPS identify and evaluate potential risks so that countermeasures can be recommended to help prevent or mitigate risks. FPS inspectors are law enforcement officers and trained security experts who perform facility security assessments and inspections and respond to

---

[10]ISC, *Physical Security Criteria for Federal Facilities: An Interagency Security Committee Standard.* According to ISC, its 2013 guidance on occupant emergency programs incorporates all 10 minimum OEP elements.

[11]The White House, Presidential Policy Directive 21, *Critical Infrastructure Security and Resilience* (Washington, D.C.: Feb. 12, 2013). This directive establishes national policy for critical infrastructure and, among other things, assigns roles and responsibilities to specific federal agencies for different critical infrastructure sectors.

[12]See 41 C.F.R. §§ 102-74.230 to .260.

[13]ISC, *Occupant Emergency Programs: An Interagency Security Committee Guide.*

[14]6 U.S.C. § 203(3); 40 U.S.C. § 1315.

[15]Memorandum of Agreement between the Department of Homeland Security and the General Services Administration, June 8, 2006.

incidents. FPS also assigns an FSL in accordance with the ISC standard and in coordination with the FSC and GSA representative based on a facility's cumulative rating on five factors established by ISC (plus an adjustment for intangible factors), as shown in figure 1. According to ISC, a facility's FSL is a key factor in establishing appropriate physical security measures. Further, while the minimum OEP elements in the ISC 2010 standard apply to all FSL facilities, what is appropriate may vary based on facility characteristics.

Figure 1: Facility Security Level Factors and Facility Security Level

Factor	Points				Score
	1	**2**	**3**	**4**	
Mission criticality	Low	Medium	High	Very high	
Symbolism	Low	Medium	High	Very high	
Facility population	100 or less	101-250	251-750	More than 750	
Facility size	10,000 or less sq. ft.	10,001 to 100,000 sq. ft.	100,001 to 250,000 sq. ft	More than 250,000 sq. ft	
Threat to tenant	Low	Medium	High	Very high	
					Sum of above
Facility security level (FSL)	I 5-7 points	II 8-12 points	III 13-17 points	IV 18 or more points	Preliminary FSL
Intangible adjustment	Justification for intangible adjustment				+/- 1 FSL
					Final FSL

Source: Interagency Security Committee and GAO

Individual Agencies Are Responsible for Developing and Maintaining OEPs, and the Majority of Selected Facilities' OEPs Generally Reflect Federal Guidance

The federal agencies that occupy federal facilities are responsible for preparing and maintaining OEPs; ISC, GSA, and FPS provide guidance or assistance to the agencies in developing OEPs, and FPS can periodically review OEPs. All 20 facilities we visited had written emergency plans in place, the majority of which reflected ISC's minimum elements for a facility OEP. The OEPs we reviewed varied in length and content based on a number of factors, such as facility security level.

Agencies Are Responsible for OEPs with Assistance from ISC, GSA, and FPS

Ensuring that each of the approximately 9,600 GSA-owned and -leased facilities protected by FPS has emergency plans to safely evacuate occupants is a complex undertaking. Each agency occupying a facility is responsible for ensuring the safety of its occupants in that facility. Although no one agency accounts for OEPs across the federal government, ISC, GSA, and FPS each provide guidance on what should be included in a plan. FPS also provides a check that plans are in place as part of its periodic facility security assessments.

Federal Agencies' Responsibilities

Federal agencies have designated officials to create and oversee emergency plans and duties for the facilities they occupy. According to federal regulations, designated officials are responsible for developing, implementing, and maintaining the OEP for the facility.[16] In the event of an emergency, the designated official is expected to initiate appropriate action according to the OEP, including the evacuation and relocation of facility occupants. The designated official is also to establish, staff, and train an Occupant Emergency Organization, which is to be composed of employees from within agencies designated to perform the requirements established by the plan. We found that all 20 facilities we visited had assigned designated officials to perform these duties.

ISC Involvement

ISC is responsible for issuing policies and standards on facility protection, such as OEPs, but does not review the extent to which federal facilities have OEPs. As previously mentioned, ISC listed 10 minimum elements in

---

[16]41 C.F.R. § 102-74.230.

its ISC 2010 standard that an OEP should address.[17] In March 2013, ISC issued *Occupant Emergency Programs: An Interagency Security Committee Guide,* to further assist department and agency officials as they develop and review their occupant emergency programs, including how to develop OEPs that best fit their individual facility and agency needs.[18] According to ISC officials, the guidance was disseminated via e-mail to the full ISC membership, which includes 53 federal agencies and departments. ISC officials said they rely on agencies located in federal facilities to ensure OEPs are in place and shared several reasons why it would not be feasible for ISC to comprehensively review OEPs. First, according to these officials, ISC decided to use broad guidelines that would allow agencies to develop plans that are suited to the unique characteristics of their facilities. As a result, the guidance does not provide specific standards or metrics against which to compare a facility's plan. Second, although OEPs are an important part of an overall occupant emergency program, ISC officials said that OEPs are a relatively small part of an agency's overall emergency and security planning, which may not warrant implementing additional monitoring and data-gathering efforts. Last, ISC officials cited staffing constraints and noted that, per Executive Order 12977, they rely on volunteers from member organizations to carry out the committee's efforts.

GSA Involvement

GSA also plays a role in coordinating directly with facilities to provide guidance on OEPs and participates in emergency planning efforts. According to GSA officials, its tenant agencies, through their designated officials, are responsible for tracking and reviewing OEPs. Further, designated officials are to represent the government's interests to public safety and emergency response in conjunction with GSA and other key stakeholders. However, GSA officials said that they will assist agencies with OEPs as requested. GSA officials also told us that they participate on facility security committees and in planning drills and exercises, and can provide GSA and other OEP guidance to their tenants. GSA officials also said that they work with tenants, as well as building owners at leased facilities, to ensure that facilities comply with building safety codes, such as having appropriate exits and fire alarms.[19] Presidential Policy Directive

---

[17]ISC, *Physical Security Criteria for Federal Facilities: An Interagency Security Committee Standard.*

[18]ISC, *Occupant Emergency Programs: An Interagency Security Committee Guide.*

[19]See 41 C.F.R § 102-74.360.

21 jointly assigns FPS and GSA responsibility for critical infrastructure protection of the government facilities sector.[20] According to a GSA Associate Administrator, there is a need for greater visibility of OEPs. Consequently, GSA and FPS officials told us they have initiated discussions on future collaboration to ensure OEPs are in place and updated at GSA facilities. According to GSA officials, as part of a Joint Strategy for Facility Resilience, GSA and FPS will work collaboratively to develop a platform that could serve as a repository for OEPs, facility security assessments, and other data over the next 2 to 4 years.

FPS Involvement

FPS is responsible for assisting federal agencies with guidance, training, exercises, and drills, and also conducts periodic facility security assessments that include checking OEPs. FPS officials in the three cities we visited said that, when requested, they provide agencies with OEP guidance, which includes an OEP template, and advise the designated and other agency officials regarding an emergency plan that is appropriate for their location and circumstances. According to FPS officials, its OEP template (a Microsoft Word file) can be requested from the DHS and GSA websites and can also be made available to agency officials on a DVD. Of the 20 facilities we visited, officials at 14 reported using FPS guidance or feedback on their OEPs, for example, using the FPS template as a base for their OEPs and officials at 5 facilities reported using their own agency guidance for OEP development. FPS officials in one city we visited reiterated that some agencies have their own emergency coordinators and choose not to use FPS materials. Officials at 1 facility reported not using FPS or other agency guidance for OEP development.

FPS also provides evacuation training, including awareness training on active shooter and workplace violence incidents,[21] as well as safety and security.[22] Officials from 5 of the 20 facilities we visited mentioned specific training FPS had provided them, primarily active shooter awareness

---

[20]The White House, PPD 21: *Critical Infrastructure Security and Resilience.*

[21]An active shooter is an individual actively engaged in killing or attempting to kill people in a confined and populated area.

[22]According to the memorandum of agreement between DHS and GSA, DHS will provide training as requested on the basic concepts and procedures of an OEP and update the OEP guidance as necessary. FPS does not track delivery of all training provided at facilities for all regions.

training, and officials at 1 facility stated that they were planning an active shooter exercise with FPS.

Additionally, FPS inspectors in the three locations we visited said they make themselves available to participate in facility exercises and emergency drills, and officials at 11 of the 20 facilities we visited told us that FPS had participated, for example, by providing traffic control services or ensuring all occupants have evacuated. Officials at 5 facilities we visited mentioned that FPS had not consistently participated in drills at their facilities, in one case because FPS had not been invited and in another case because FPS arrived after the drill had been completed.[23] According to FPS officials, FPS participation in exercises and drills can be limited if FPS personnel are not nearby, are on duty responding to actual incidents, or were not given advance notice.

FPS inspectors also are to check and answer a series of questions about the facility's OEP during periodic facility security assessments, including whether or not the facility has a written OEP, and consider whether it addresses the 10 minimum elements for an OEP identified by ISC. FPS's facility security assessments are to occur periodically, every 3 to 5 years, depending on the security level of the facility.[24] In July 2011, we reported that FPS could not complete security assessments as intended because of limitations in its assessment tool, among other reasons.[25] We recommended that the agency evaluate whether other alternatives for completing security assessments would be more appropriate. DHS agreed with the recommendation and has developed a new facility security assessment tool, the Modified Infrastructure Survey Tool (MIST), which DHS officials said was deployed in April 2012. FPS headquarters officials told us that its agency currently has no national data on which agencies have an OEP, and we previously reported that MIST was not designed to compare risk across federal facilities.[26] FPS headquarters officials said as the agency moves forward with enhancing MIST's

---

[23]Officials in the remaining 4 facilities did not provide information on whether FPS participated in drills or exercises.

[24]Facility security assessments are to be conducted at least every 5 years for level I and II facilities and at least every 3 years for level III and IV facilities.

[25]GAO-11-705R.

[26]GAO, *Federal Protective Service: Actions Needed to Assess Risk and Better Manage Contract Guards at Federal Facilities*, GAO-12-739 (Washington, D.C.: Aug. 10, 2012).

capabilities, it would consider whether it was feasible to add a feature that would allow it to aggregate data across facilities, such as the status of OEPs.

According to FPS officials, recommendations about OEPs and evacuation processes, such as suggestions to change assembly points in the event of an evacuation, may be made during facility security assessments. For example, one FPS inspector recommended that 1 facility change its assembly point because he determined that it was too close to the evacuated facility. Although officials at this facility expressed some reluctance in changing the assembly location, the inspector told us that facilities generally implement FPS suggestions. FPS inspectors also said that there have been few examples where agencies did not want to comply. Although agencies do not have to comply with their recommendations on OEPs, FPS inspectors stated that they do have enforcement authority related to life safety issues during an actual emergency event, such as moving occupants to different evacuation locations. Further, FPS headquarters officials said recommendations about OEPs may be made at any time, not just during facility security assessments.

The Majority of Selected Facilities' OEPs Generally Reflect Federal Guidance

All 20 facilities we visited had written OEPs, as required by regulation, which included evacuation procedures. Consistent with the ISC 2010 standard that plans should be reviewed annually, officials at 19 of the 20 facilities we visited reported that they review, and update as needed, their emergency plans on at least an annual basis, and some reported reviewing their plans more frequently. For example, officials at 1 FSL-II facility reported that the OEP program manager reviews the plan on a monthly basis, and officials at a FSL-IV facility said their plan was reviewed quarterly. The OEPs we examined had been reviewed by officials in the past year, except for one. Officials at this FSL-III facility reported that they have an emergency plan in place; however, their OEP had not been annually reviewed, and was last updated in 2004. Officials at that facility said that a revision was currently under way. Officials at all 20 facilities told us they conduct at least one annual evacuation drill, as directed in the ISC 2010 standard, with several officials reporting their facility conducts multiple drills each year.

We analyzed the extent to which the selected facilities' OEPs incorporated elements that should be in an OEP according to the ISC 2010 standard, which outlines 10 minimum elements:

1. purpose and circumstances for activation,

2. command officials and supporting personnel contact information,

3. occupant life safety options (e.g., evacuation, shelter-in-place),

4. local law enforcement and first responder response,

5. special needs individuals (e.g., those with disabilities, or who are deaf),

6. visitors,

7. special facilities (e.g., child care centers),

8. assembly and accountability,

9. security during and after incident, and

10. training and exercises.

We found that 13 of the 20 facilities addressed all of the minimum elements that were applicable; in some of these cases, OEP elements were addressed in other emergency documents, such as supplemental child care OEPs.[27] Seven of the facilities did not address at least one OEP element in the ISC 2010 standard in their OEPs or other documents. That an element was not in the plan or in related documents for 7 facilities does not necessarily indicate potential vulnerabilities for these facilities because other procedures or facility services may address the intent of the OEP element. For example, 6 of the 7 OEPs did not specifically describe security during or after an emergency event.[28] Officials in all six cases identified existing security, such as building security guards, as having responsibility. Officials at 2 facilities reported that they were updating their OEPs after our site visit and would identify existing security in the plans. As another example, at 2 facilities where training or exercises were not included in the OEPs, officials at both facilities (which were housed in leased GSA space) said that building management conducts drills and that they participate. The 2010 standard and 2013 ISC

---

[27]Not all elements were applicable for all facilities, for example, some facilities did not have an associated special facility. For applicable elements in other documents, we verified that the element was in other emergency documents. ISC's 2010 standard on OEP minimum elements does not explicitly require that OEP elements be addressed in a single document.

[28]The ISC guidance does not provide a further description of what this or the other 9 elements should contain. In our review we looked for any general reference to security during or after an emergency event.

guidance both allow for necessary adjustments to be made to a facility's emergency plan based on specific requirements or needs.

Selected OEPs Varied Based on a Number of Factors, Consistent with the ISC Standard

Plans at the 20 facilities we reviewed were unique to each facility, and there were differences in how each element was addressed, as the ISC 2010 standard and 2013 guidance allow. Specific details on how OEP elements are expected to be addressed are not included in ISC's 2010 standard, which we used to review facility OEPs, or in ISC's 2013 guidance. ISC officials said that there is so much variability among facilities that it is difficult to identify what would be appropriate for all facilities.[29] For example, in one plan, command official information might include multiple contacts and a detailed list of responsibilities for each official, while another plan refers occupants to security services, which would be responsible for contacting command officials. Appendix II provides other examples of variation in how facilities addressed the 10 minimum elements in the plans we reviewed.

We did observe some commonality in the 20 facility OEPs we reviewed, based on facility characteristics such as security level, whether the facility was GSA owned or leased, and occupant characteristics, as shown in table 1.

---

[29]Consistent with ISC's approach, FPS (in its protocol for review of OEPs during a facility security assessment) notes that the scope and complexity of the OEP are dependent on the facility's size, population, and mission.

Table 1: Our Analysis of 20 Selected Occupant Emergency Plan (OEP) Features and Selected Facility Characteristics

Facility characteristics	OEP features
Facility security level	The 9 FSL-IV facilities we reviewed were larger facilities and had more detailed emergency plans than the 6 FSL-II, smaller facilities. For example, 1 FSL-IV facility developed a 56-page OEP, a child care center OEP supplement, and an OEP flip chart that each employee is to receive, whereas 1 FSL-II facility had an abbreviated six-page OEP.[a]
	For the 20 OEPs we reviewed, larger facilities with more occupants tended to have a more detailed structure for assembly and accountability during an evacuation than did smaller facilities, for example, establishing specific positions such an assembly area monitor to communicate with the command center. At smaller facilities, facility plans identified the heads of operating units, managers, and supervisors as responsible for staff accountability in an emergency situation.
Facility is owned or leased	ISC's 2010 standard and 2013 guidance apply to both owned and leased GSA facilities. All 6 of the FSL-II facilities, 4 of the 5 FSL-III facilities, and 1 of the 9 FSL-IV facilities that we met with—in total 11 of the 20—were in leased space. (Ninety-three percent of all GSA office facilities are in leased space.) Officials at 2 facilities that were tenants in leased commercial space reported that they rely in part on emergency plans developed by the building management for evacuation purposes. For example, 1 facility had an emergency plan that descr bed evacuation procedures, but officials explained that the circumstances that would call for an evacuation were outlined in the lessor's building emergency plan.
	In 7of the 9 GSA-owned facilities we visited, officials reported having facility security committees that are to play a role in the development and maintenance of the facility OEP, whereas none of the officials in the 11 leased facilities reported having a facility security committee.
Occupant characteristics	Occupant characteristics were also a factor in OEP content in the 20 OEPs we analyzed. Facilities with visitors had plans that addressed visitor evacuation needs, whereas those with few or no visitors did not emphasize this element in their plans. For example, officials at 1 FSL-IV facility said visitors are rare, while officials at another FSL-IV facility said they have over 1,000 visitors to the facility each day, and contract guards help ensure their safety. At least 2 facilities supplemented their OEPs by providing brochures containing evacuation information to visitors.
	Facility plans we analyzed also reflected provisions for persons with disabilities. Officials at 1 of the 3 facilities where the OEP did not include provisions for persons with special needs reported that they did not have special need occupants at the facility.

Source: GAO analysis of facility OEPs.

[a]GSA allows the use of an abbreviated OEP for its' small ,storefront facilities.

A Majority of Officials in Our Review Reported Responding to Challenges Identified during Their Facility Drills and Evacuations

Officials at 14 of 20 facilities in our review identified challenges, and all but one reported responding to challenges they encountered in developing and implementing emergency evacuation procedures.[30] Officials at 6 facilities said that they did not identify any challenges. Half of the officials reporting challenges told us that actual emergency events and exercises helped to identify issues and mitigation steps that allowed their facilities to generally carry out effective emergency evacuations. For example, the majority of officials at facilities we visited in Washington, D.C., who experienced the 2011 earthquake said that because of the lack of earthquake procedures or training, emergency teams could not control employees' evacuation process. They said that many employees essentially self-evacuated, exposing themselves to hazards such as falling debris and, in one case, evacuated to an unsafe assembly area under an overpass. These officials said that they have since researched proper earthquake procedures, and have revised or are in the process of revising their OEPs accordingly.

As shown in figure 2, officials at facilities we visited identified several challenges they addressed. The top three challenges cited by officials at the14 selected facilities that identified challenges were (1) participation apathy (10 facilities),[31] (2) knowing which employees are present (9 facilities), and (3) keeping plan information current (7 facilities). The remaining challenges were cited by 6 or fewer of the selected facilities.[32]

---

[30]Officials at facilities we visited determined whether they perceived an issue to be a challenge or not. We asked officials at all 20 facilities if they experienced specific challenges. In addition, officials in all but 1 of the 14 facilities with challenges provided additional information on actions taken to mitigate the challenges, which we include as examples.

[31]For purposes of this report, we used "participation apathy" to refer to what various officials described as employees unwillingness or lack of interest in participating in emergency drills or as members of an emergency team.

[32]Officials at 11 facilities reported addressing more than one challenge.

Figure 2: Evacuation Challenges Identified by 20 Selected Federal Facilities

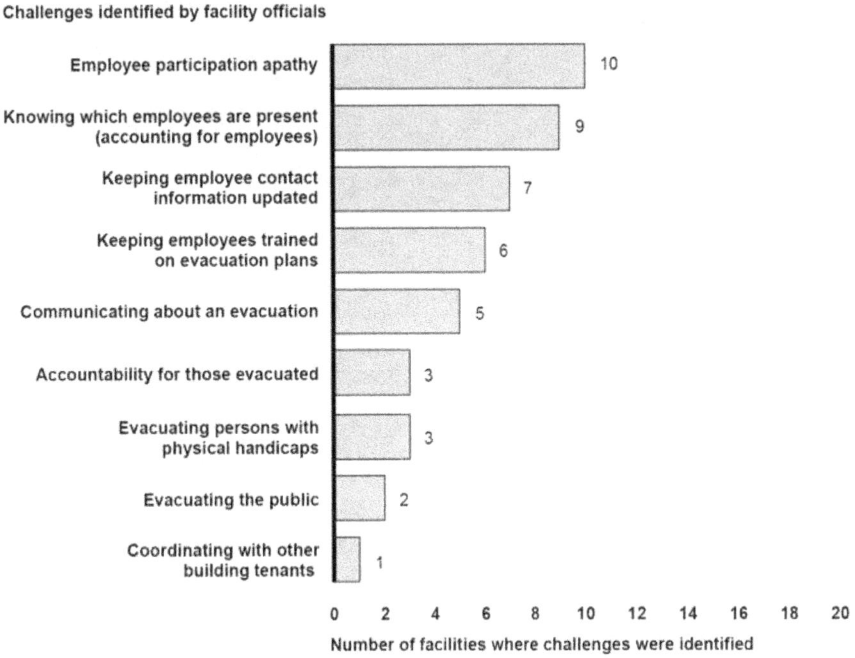

Challenges identified by facility officials

Number of facilities where challenges were identified

Source: GAO analysis of challenges identified by facility officials.

Officials at all but 1 facility provided additional detail regarding actions they are taking to mitigate facility evacuation challenges. Officials at that facility reported that the OEP was to be updated, but did not describe how they specifically plan to mitigate OEP challenges they identified.[33]

For each of the top three challenges, officials at facilities that cited challenges described some of the actions taken to address those challenges.

- **Employee participation apathy.** Officials at 10 of the 20 selected facilities cited apathy as a challenge they encountered, such as employees not participating in or responding quickly to drills; not wanting to stop working or leave the building; not reporting to the assembly area (e.g., going for a coffee break during an evacuation

---

[33]Officials at this facility identified four challenges, which are the same top four challenges that were identified by the 20 facilities overall, as shown in figure 2.

GAO-14-101 Federal Facility Evacuations

drill); and not volunteering for emergency team responsibilities, such as becoming a floor warden. Officials at 9 of the 10 facilities described a variety of actions to address this challenge, Officials at 5 facilities said that leadership plays a role, such as leading by example, or drawing management or supervisory attention to nonparticipants. For example, at 1 facility, officials said supervisors were notified of the lack of participation in emergency drills and training and asked to emphasize the importance of participation. Officials at another facility indicated that senior leaders lead by example, responding quickly and taking emergency drills and participation seriously to encourage employees to take emergency responsibilities seriously. Officials at 3 facilities said they address apathy by using drills, an awareness campaign, or other efforts to promote participation. At the other 2 facilities where this challenge was identified, officials at 1 facility said they were reviewing challenges and action options, and the other did not provide information on any mitigating activities. Officials at the third facility said that they made efforts to make emergency and evacuation training more interesting and interactive to maintain employee interest and attention, such as implementing a game meant to teach about various emergency situations and proper procedures.

- **Knowing which employees are present (accounting for employees).** Officials at 9 of the 20 selected facilities reported encountering this challenge, with employees teleworking or working offsite as a contributing factor. Officials at 8 facilities provided various examples of addressing this challenge. At 6 facilities, officials said they relied on supervisors, managers, and sign-in sheets to keep track of employees. Officials at 2 facilities mentioned using or planning to use technology to account for employees in an emergency situation. One facility is developing an emergency notification system that sends emergency information to as many as 10 different electronic devices to contact an individual and determine the individual's location. Another facility is planning to use an entry scan system that records who is in the building and can provide a list to take roll at the evacuation rally point to account for employees. At 1 facility, where officials reported they are updating their OEP, efforts to mitigate this challenge were not described.

- **Keeping emergency contact information updated.** Officials at 7 of the 20 facilities said that it was an ongoing challenge to keep emergency contacts in the OEP current because of changes in an employee's contact information or status such as a transfer or retirement. To address this challenge, officials at 6 facilities said they review and update contact information at various points, such as when staff leave; before drills; or on a daily, weekly, monthly, or quarterly basis at different facilities. At one facility, officials said that they rely on tenants to provide notice of personnel changes. At another, an official said that the facility's technology department was able to align its employee finder database with the agency's separation database to automatically flag when employees have a change in location or status. Information was not available for 1 facility on any efforts to mitigate this challenge.

Officials at facilities we visited reported experiencing and addressing other challenges less frequently such as keeping employees trained, evacuating the public and persons with physical handicaps, communicating about an evacuation, and coordinating with other building tenants. Officials who reported encountering these challenges told us that they had mechanisms in place to mitigate the challenges they encountered, such as the use of hand-held radios for communications, so the challenges were not considered an issue that prevented them from carrying out effective emergency evacuations.

Other incidents or situations have also prompted facilities to revise their OEPs or for FPS to evaluate emerging threats and revise its training, as discussed in the examples below.

- **Practice drills.** During a practice drill evacuation at 1 facility, it was discovered that the path to the evacuation assembly area was up a steep slope and that some of the employees could not make the climb. The assembly area was subsequently changed and the OEP revised.

- **Emerging threats.** FPS headquarters officials stated that recent media coverage of active shooter situations has increased the public's perception of this threat to facility safety and security. A fatal active shooter incident at 1 facility in Los Angeles prompted the revision of safety and evacuation procedures. FPS headquarters officials said that FPS has developed awareness training courses for how to handle an active shooter situation, and has proactively offered this training to facilities.

To identify and help agencies address evacuation or OEP challenges, officials at ISC, GSA, and FPS said that they provide initial guidance regarding the OEP, and may provide additional assistance if requested by facilities or agencies. For example, ISC officials stated that they issued their March 2013 OEP Program Guidance in response to concerns raised by ISC's members for consistency in OEP guidance. Officials said agencies experiencing a challenge regarding their OEPs (or other issues) can ask ISC for specific help such as one-on-one assistance, or referral to other agency officials that have addressed a similar challenge. Also, ISC officials said a working group can be created to identify solutions to an issue, as was the case in developing the 2013 guidance. As discussed earlier, GSA and FPS have published OEP information, and may provide additional information or training assistance in meeting specific challenges on a case-by-case basis.

Agency Comments

We provided a draft of this report to DHS and GSA for review and comment.[34] GSA had no comments on the report. DHS provided technical comments, which were incorporated as appropriate. DHS also provided written comments, which are summarized below and reprinted in appendix III.

In its written comments, DHS reiterated that OEPs are critical in safely evacuating federal facility occupants in an emergency. DHS noted that GAO recognized the complex roles performed by the ISC, GSA, FPS, and agency officials to ensure that the approximately 9,600 GSA-owned and -leased facilities have an OEP. For instance, DHS cited that ISC establishes standards and guidance for developing OEPs that are responsive to individual facility needs, whereas FPS is responsible for coordinating with and assisting department and agency officials in developing facility OEPs, and providing agencies with evacuation training, among other things. DHS also stated that it is committed to working collaboratively with ISC and GSA to identify and mitigate security-related vulnerabilities at federal facilities.

We are sending copies of this report to the Department of Homeland Security, the Administrator of the General Services Administration, selected congressional committees, and other interested parties. In addition, the report is available at no charge on the GAO website at http://www.gao.gov.

Should you or your staff have any questions concerning this report, please contact Joseph Kirschbaum at (202) 512-9971 or by e-mail at

---

[34]Agency comments were made on GAO-13-706. This report number was subsequently changed to GAO-14-101.

GAO-14-101 Federal Facility Evacuations

kirschbaumj@gao.gov or Mark Goldstein at (202) 512-2834 or goldsteinm@gao.gov. Contact points for our Offices of Congressional Relations and Public Affairs may be found on the last page of this report. Key contributors to this report are listed in appendix IV.

Sincerely yours,

Joseph Kirschbaum
Acting Director, Homeland Security and Justice

Mark Goldstein
Director, Physical Infrastructure

Appendix I: Objectives, Scope, and Methodology

This report describes

1. who is responsible for ensuring that federal facilities have occupant emergency plans (OEP) in place and the extent to which selected facilities' OEPs reflect federal guidance and

2. evacuation challenges, if any, that selected facilities experienced and what actions, if any, they reported taking to address these issues.

To describe who is responsible for ensuring that federal facilities have OEPs in place, we reviewed federal laws, regulations, executive orders, and guidance related to the oversight of federal facilities. This included relevant sections of the Homeland Security Act of 2002; the regulations regarding federal property facility management and federal agency requirements for OEPs; Executive Order 12977, establishing the Interagency Security Committee (ISC); and Executive Order 13286, amending it.[1] We reviewed OEP guidance issued by ISC, the Federal Protective Service (FPS), and the General Services Administration (GSA).[2] We also reviewed our previous work on the roles of FPS, GSA, and ISC in protecting federal facilities.[3] We interviewed relevant senior agency officials regarding their agencies' role in ensuring federal facilities have OEPs in place, including ISC officials in Washington, D.C.; officials from FPS and GSA in their headquarters; and FPS and GSA officials in the three field locations where we conducted site visits to selected federal facilities, as described below.

---

[1]Pub. L. No. 107-296, 116 Stat. 2135; 41 C.F.R. pt. 102-74; Exec. Order No. 12,977, 60 Fed. Reg. 54,411 (Oct. 19, 1995); Exec. Order No. 13,286, 68 Fed. Reg. 10,619 (Feb. 28, 2003).

[2]Among others, guidance we reviewed included: ISC, *Physical Security Criteria for Federal Facilities: An Interagency Security Committee Standard* (Washington, D.C.: Apr. 12, 2010), and *Occupant Emergency Programs: An Interagency Security Committee Guide* (Washington, D.C.: March 2013); FPS, *Secure Facilities, Safe Occupants– Occupant Emergency Plans: Development, Implementation and Maintenance*, Updated May 2010, and related supplements (Washington, D.C.); and GSA Public Buildings Service, *Occupant Emergency Program Guide* (Washington D.C.: 2002).

[3]GAO, *Federal Real Property Security: Interagency Security Committee Should Implement a Lessons-Learned Process*, GAO-12-901 (Washington, D.C.: Sept. 10, 2012); *Federal Protective Service: Actions Needed to Resolve Delays and Inadequate Oversight Issues with FPS's Risk Assessment and Management Program*, GAO-11-705R (Washington, D.C.: July 15, 2011); and *Homeland Security: Greater Attention to Key Practices Would Improve the Federal Protective Service's Approach to Facility Protection*, GAO-10-142 (Washington, D.C.: Oct. 23, 2009).

To describe the extent to which the selected facilities' OEPs reflect
federal guidance, we conducted site visits at 20 of the GSA facilities
protected by FPS.[4] We selected a nonprobability sample of facilities as
follows:

- We selected three geographically diverse areas with a concentration
  of GSA facilities from GSA's top 15 major real estate markets.
  Specifically, we selected two areas from the top 5 markets in terms of
  GSA assets (Los Angeles, California, and Washington, D.C.), and one
  area from a smaller GSA market defined as having fewer than 100
  facilities (Kansas City, Missouri).

- To ensure a subset of facilities would be able to discuss evacuation
  experiences they have had, we selected 9 facilities total from the
  three areas that had reported an evacuation incident to an FPS
  MegaCenter during 2011 or 2012. Each of the four FPS MegaCenters
  records incidents such as fire alarms, suspicious packages, and
  evacuation drills that are reported to that center as part of the center's
  operations log, with an activity code that can be queried for incidents.
  Only incidents reported to a MegaCenter are captured, so, for
  example, if local police respond to a call at a facility and do not call
  FPS, the incident would not be included in the MegaCenter data.
  According to discussions with MegaCenter data officials and a review
  of the data content, we determined that the incident data were reliable
  for our purposes, as our sample was not intended to be representative
  of all incidents.[5]

- We used a list provided by GSA from its Real Estate Across the
  United States (REXUS) database to select the remaining 11 facilities
  to provide a mix of owned and leased properties, and a mix of facility
  security levels. We determined that the REXUS database was reliable
  for our purposes based on a review of database documents and

[4]GSA reported having over 9,600 assets, or 11 percent of all federal square footage, as of
September 2011, which includes office buildings, courthouses, warehouses, laboratories,
parking lots, and other properties. We limited our facility selection to the almost 7,900
GSA office buildings, of which 7,301 are office spaces that GSA leases. For the purposes
of this report, we used the term "facilities" to descr be the 20 GSA assets in our sample.

[5]In addition to the 9 facilities we selected using the incident data, officials at an additional
7 facilities reported during our interviews that they had evacuated in the last 3 years, for a
total of 16 facilities with evacuation experience.

discussion with relevant GSA officials. See table 2 for a summary of
characteristics of the 20 facilities we selected.

Table 2: Selected Facility Characteristics of the 20 Case Study Facilities in Our
Review

	Washington, D.C.	Kansas City, Missouri	Los Angeles, California	Total
Total facilities	6	7	7	20
Facility security level (FSL)[a]				
FSL-IV	3	3	3	9
FSL-III	2	1	2	5
FSL-II	1	3	2	6
Facilities reporting they evacuated in the last 3 years	6	5	5	16
General Service Administration (GSA)–owned facilities	4	2	3	9
GSA-leased facilities	2	5	4	11

Source: GAO analysis of selected facility characteristics.

[a]A FSL of I to V is assigned by FPS to facilities it protects. A higher-numbered FSL facility would be
considered a facility with a higher security risk than a facility with a lower number.

For all selected facilities, we reviewed the extent to which the OEPs
included the 10 minimum elements that should be included based on
ISC's Physical Security Standard (ISC 2010 standard) for federal
facilities.[6] For example, 1 element that an OEP should include is
information on "Special Needs Individuals (disabled, deaf, etc.)." For each
facility in our sample, two team members reviewed the OEP and
assessed whether or not each of the elements was addressed. The ISC
2010 standard indicates that the 10 elements should be present;
however, it notes that the scope and complexity of the OEP are
dependent on the facility's size, population, and mission, and the
standard does not provide a description of, or detail on, what should be
included for each element. Further, not all elements may be applicable for

---

[6]ISC, April 12, 2010. We used the ISC 2010 list of OEP elements because ISC's March
2013 guidance was not finalized when we conducted our work, or when the plans we
reviewed were developed. Officials said the 2010 elements are incorporated in the 2013
guidance.

a facility, for example, if the facility does not have a child care or other special facility.[7] Because of the general nature of the elements, we assessed whether a particular element was present in a facility's OEP, not its quality or comprehensiveness. We reviewed additional documents provided by agency officials, such as child care center emergency plans, emergency cards for quick use, and FPS's facility security assessment protocol, used by FPS inspectors when periodically checking OEPs.[8] We also interviewed GSA property managers and officials from agencies who occupy each facility about the facility's plan. Further, those officials were those identified by GSA and the tenant agency as most knowledgeable about the OEP, which in some cases was the designated official, and in other cases, the facility official was, for example, a manager involved with facility security. While the findings from our 20 case studies are not generalizable to all GSA-owned and -leased facilities, they provide specific examples of how selected facilities have addressed emergency plan requirements and provide insights from a range of federal facilities.

To describe the challenges and evacuation experiences of the 20 selected facilities, we discussed specific evacuation instances with facility and GSA officials, the challenges officials face in planning and executing evacuation plans, and any steps taken to mitigate the challenges. We asked about evacuation challenges in general, and about specific challenges that were identified by a review of the literature and from discussion with FPS. We also asked officials at the facilities we visited about challenges, and they determined whether they perceived an issue to be a challenge or not. Where available, we reviewed after-action reports documenting facility evacuation experiences. We also discussed evacuation experiences and challenges with ISC, GSA, and FPS officials. Our findings regarding what issues presented challenges and how such challenges could be resolved cannot be generalized to all GSA-owned and -leased facilities; however, they provide specific examples of issues encountered and how varying facilities addressed them.

---

[7]In instances where a particular element was not applicable, but the OEP had all other elements, we considered the OEP as addressing all applicable elements.

[8]Department of Homeland Security, *Federal Protective Service Modified Infrastructure Survey Tool; Security Management Profile*, (Washington, D.C.: March, 2012) (Official use only.)

We conducted this performance audit from August 2012 to October 2013 in accordance with generally accepted government auditing standards. Those standards require that we plan and perform the audit to obtain sufficient, appropriate evidence to provide a reasonable basis for our findings and conclusions based on our audit objectives. We believe that the evidence obtained provides a reasonable basis for our findings and conclusions based on our audit objectives.

Appendix II: Examples of How OEP Elements Were Included in 20 Selected Facilities' Emergency Plans

Facility plans we reviewed addressed the ISC minimum 10 elements in a variety of ways, consistent with agency guidance and facility characteristics. Guidance in the ISC 2010 Physical Security Criteria for Federal Facilities notes that an OEP's scope and complexity will be dependent on a facility's size, population, and mission.[1] Table 3 presents excerpts from OEPs from the 20 selected facilities we visited in Washington, D.C.; Kansas City, Missouri; and Los Angeles, California; and were selected to show the variation in how plan elements were addressed.

Table 3: How Selected Facility Occupant Emergency Plans (OEP) Addressed Interagency Security Committee OEP Elements

Purpose and circumstance

- Purpose: "This OEP and support documents are intended to foster pre-planning knowledge, training and rehearsal, so consequences of emergency events may be mitigated." Activation: "The Occupant Emergency Plan may be activated when an emergency situation occurs. Typical emergency events, which could cause activation, are fire, chemical spill, tornado, earthquake, and radiological contamination, among others." **(FSL-III)**[a]
- Purpose: "This plan directs the implementation of an incident command system, notification of (agency) and local emergency officials, building evacuation, shelter in place actions, active shooter procedures, and a personnel accountability system in the event of a suspected or actual emergency at (facility)." Activation: "Any incident that may present an immediate danger to the life and health of an individual, or multiple occupants.... These incidents include vis ble fire or smoke conditions, emergent sick or injured employees, explosions, gun fire, "active shooter incidents," assaults (in progress), and hostage situations. **(FSL-IV)**

Command officials and supporting personnel contact information

- The OEP identifies the titles, names, and numbers for the OEP organization including the designated official, occupant emergency coordinator, floor team coordinator, and so forth and alternates for each position. **(FSL-IV)**
- "The Occupant Emergency Team structure is consistent with the incident command system and National Incident Management System." The OEP provides team member positions, office and cell phone contacts, and team member responsibilities. **(FSL-III)**

Occupant life-safety options (evacuation, shelter in place)

- The OEP covers partial evacuations, full evacuations, shelter in place, areas of assembly, specific emergency situations, and the roles of emergency evacuation team members. **(FSL-II)**
- The OEP specifies the methods by which total or selective evacuation will take place, which can be the result of many situations (fire, bomb threat, or other emergencies) that mandate clearing the facility, and describes situations that would require employees to shelter in place. **(FSL-IV)**

Local law enforcement and first responder response (coordination and contact information)

- The OEP states that communications with government agencies, community organizations, and utilities are important in orchestrating an effective emergency response strategy, and lists those entities with contact information. (e.g., Washington, D.C., Police Department, local hospitals). **(FSL-IV)**
- The OEP includes contact information for local police; fire, and the Federal Protective Service officials said that FPS will notify local law enforcement in an emergency, and that FPS has memorandums of agreement in place with local police, sheriffs, and the highway patrol. **(FSL-IV)**

---

[1]An Interagency Security Committee Standard, April 12, 2010.

Purpose and circumstance

Evacuating special needs individuals (disabled, deaf, etc.)

- The facility utilizes guidelines of the U.S. Equal Employment Opportunity Commission (EEOC) on emergency evacuation procedures for special needs employees. However, all employees with special needs must take personal responsibility to notify and consult with their supervisors of their special needs before an emergency occurs. **(FSL-IV)**
- The OEP designates an employee with disabilities monitor who is responsible for establishing a predesignated location, such as the nearest stairwell, to meet the assigned monitor during an alarm. The OEP provide guidelines for the monitor, who is responsible for remaining with the employee at the predesignated area. The monitor is also responsible for using the evacuation chair to evacuate the employee if possible. **(FSL-II)**

Visitors (public and contractors)

- Officials at 1 facility we visited said that the facility hosts over 1,000 visitors per day. The OEP "applies to all employees, contractors and visitors" and "If an employee or contractor has a visitor, or is the host of a meeting or briefing with visitors, then they are responsible for the safety and security of their visitors." **(FSL-IV)**
- The OEP states that it applies to all employees, support contractors, and visitors occupying the facility, and that employees are responsible for escorting their guests, visitors, and vendors out of the building. If there is a shelter-in-place emergency situation, the OEP says that if there are customers, clients, or visitors in the building, provide for their safety by asking them to stay—not leave. **(FSL-II)**

Special facilities (e.g., sensitive information facilities, child care centers)

- "Each staff member shall be assigned a specific group of children for whom he or she is to be responsible during an emergency. Center staff should conduct practice drills over the prescribed evacuation routes so children will not be unprepared or unduly alarmed should a real emergency occur." The OEP assigns a specific guard post to escort staff and children in an emergency. **(FSL-IV)**
- The OEP addresses Classified National Security Information and Sensitive Compartmented Information Facilities. "Upon receiving a report of fire or emergency activation, employees working with classified material shall, if safe to do so, secure classified material properly before exiting. This would include securing electronic media, paperwork, etc. in a GSA-Approved storage container. Close and properly lock all containers. Close doors and engage the intrusion detection system on your way out." **(FSL-IV)**

Assembly and accountability (staging and tracking of employees in identified area)

- The OEP provides for primary and alternate assembly areas, and identifies the designated official as responsible for accounting for all employees. After accounting for all employees, the designated official will contact the appropriate emergency personnel identified in the plan. Upon arrival of law enforcement personnel, responsibility for assembly and accountability is turned over to law enforcement officials. All employees are directed to wait for instructions and the all-clear signal. **(FSL-II)**
- Office managers should select an official rendezvous area from one of the designated assembly areas. They must then advise their employees which designated assembly area they have selected. Officials at this facility told us that the facility had multiple evacuation assembly points and changed the locations as a deterrent to possible secondary harmful actions (such as a bomb at the assembly area). Office managers are responsible for accounting for all of their employees once they have assembled at the rendezvous point at the designated assembly area. **(FSL-IV)**

Security during and after incident (protection of employees)

- The OEP delegates security during and after incidents to the facility contract security guards, and states that it is critical that security guards or law enforcement take charge of any incident that may involve physical harm. **(FSL-IV)**
- FPS provides advice and assistance, as necessary to the command team, assists in controlling building population during evacuation and subsequent reentry to the building, and provides traffic control. The facility guard post is responsible for controlling entrances and exits, as necessary. **(FSL-III)**

Purpose and circumstance

Plan specifies that emergency training or exercises be conducted

- The OEP provides that supervisors are responsible for ensuring that their staff are aware of emergency procedures and receive the necessary training. Officials at this facility told us that four drills—an evacuation, shelter in place, lockdown of the facility, and evacuation for disabled occupants—are conducted annually. **(FSL-IV)**

- The OEP indicates that managers are responsible, on a recurring basis, to discuss OEP procedures with employees, including evacuation routes, assembly points, shelter-in-place locations, assignments as special/personal assistance aids/monitors, and floor wardens/monitors they assist. **(FSL-II)**

Source: GAO analysis of selected sections of facility OEPs.

[a]FPS assigns an FSL of I to V to facilities it protects. A higher-numbered FSL facility would be considered a higher security risk than a lower-numbered FSL facility.

Appendix III: Comments from the Department of Homeland Security

Agency comments were made on GAO-13-706. This report number was subsequently changed to GAO-14-101.

U.S. Department of Homeland Security
Washington, DC 20528

September 26, 2013

Joseph Kirschbaum
Acting Director, Homeland Security and Justice
U.S. Government Accountability Office
441 G Street, NW
Washington, DC 20548

Mark Goldstein
Director, Physical Infrastructure
U.S. Government Accountability Office
441 G Street, NW
Washington, DC 20548

Re: Draft Report GAO-13-706, "FEDERAL FACILITIES: Selected Facilities' Emergency Plans Generally Reflect Federal Guidance"

Dear Sirs:

Thank you for the opportunity to review and comment on this draft report. The U.S. Department of Homeland Security (DHS) appreciates the U.S. Government Accountability Office's (GAO's) work in planning and conducting its review and issuing this report.

DHS is pleased to note GAO's recognition of the essential and complex roles performed by the Interagency Security Committee (ISC), General Services Administration (GSA) and DHS's National Protection and Program Directorate's Federal Protective Service (FPS) to ensure that each of the approximately 9,600 GSA-owned and leased facilities protected by FPS have an Occupant Emergency Plan (OEP).

FPS is responsible for providing coordination and assistance to Department and agency officials on OEP development, which includes providing an OEP template, upon request. With the assistance of FPS, federal agencies are responsible for developing and maintaining an OEP to safely evacuate occupants in the event of an emergency. These plans are critical and intended to minimize risk to personnel, property, and other assets within a facility by providing a facility-specific response plan and evacuation procedures for occupants to follow. FPS also provides agency-specific evacuation training that incorporates work place violence and active shooter awareness training. Additionally, FPS participates in drills and conducts Facility Security Assessments, which includes checking agency OEPs.

As noted in the draft report, the ISC fulfills an extremely important role in developing physical security standards. These standards, which are developed on the basis of leading security practices across the Government, set forth a decision-making process to better inform and promote consistency in the development of OEP guidance.

The ISC's 2010 Standard, "Physical Security Criteria for Federal Facilities: An Interagency Security Committee Standard," identifies 10 key elements that federal agencies should incorporate in the development of an OEP, such as the circumstances for activating the OEP. Additionally, in March 2013, the ISC issued "Occupant Emergency Programs: An Interagency Security Committee Guide" that is designed to further assist Department and agency officials with the development and review of their occupant emergency programs. These documents incorporate the use of broad guidelines that create opportunities to develop plans that are responsive to the unique characteristics of individual facilities.

DHS remains committed to continuing its collaborative work with interagency partners, specifically among ISC member agencies and GSA to identify and mitigate security related vulnerabilities at federal facilities, as appropriate.

Again, thank you for the opportunity to review and provide comment on this draft report. Technical comments were provided under separate cover. Please feel free to contact me if you have any questions. We look forward to working with you in the future.

Sincerely,

Jim H. Crumpacker
Director
Departmental GAO-OIG Liaison Office

Appendix IV: GAO Contacts and Staff Acknowledgments

GAO Contacts	Joseph Kirschbaum, 202-512-9971, or kirschbaumj@gao.gov, Mark Goldstein, 202-512-2834, or goldsteinm@gao.gov.
Staff Acknowledgments	In addition to the contacts named above, Leyla Kazaz (Assistant Director), Tammy Conquest (Assistant Director), Dorian Dunbar, Eric Hauswirth, Mary Catherine Hult, Monica Kelly, Tracey King, Erica Miles, Linda Miller, and Kelly Rubin made key contributions to this report.